Conversation with Character

By Bill & Derri Smith

A home-based language arts curriculum

With contributions by
Bethany Notgrass,
Bethany G. Smith
and
Amy J. Smith

Curriculum and aids for real life
sweethomepress.com

© 2003, 2004 Sweet Home Press

Copyright Information

Conversation with Character

Unless otherwise noted, or by unintentional omission, this publication and all its parts are property of Sweet Home Press. To reprint or otherwise use content in excess of 200 words or equal to an entire page, whichever is greater, contact us at contact@sweethomepress.com

Italicized text appearing without attribution represents statements of one or both authors, Bill and Derri Smith.

Scripture quotations are taken from the New American Standard Bible®, Copyright © 1960, 1962, 1963, 1968, 1971, 1972, 1973, 1975, 1977, 1995 by The Lockman Foundation. Used by permission. (www.Lockman.org)

© 2003, 2004 Sweet Home Press, all rights reserved

Sweet Home Press
7736 Greenbrier Road
Joelton, TN 37080
sweethomepress.com

Conversation with Character

Table of Contents

Introduction

Lessons

1. Start a Conversation
2. Pass the Ball
3. Keep an "I" Out
4. Show Interest and Effort
5. Don't Interrupt
6. Speak Blessings
7. Be Concise
8. Don't Repeat
9. Make Smooth Transitions
10. Control Body Language
11. Overcome Irritating Mannerisms
12. Don't Slam Doors
13. Be Agreeable
14. Be Loyal
15. Thank-you Pleases
16. Give and Receive Compliments
17. Take a Good Call
18. Make a Good Call
19. Water Gossip
20. End the Conversation
21. Give Respect and Honor
22. Prepare for Group-Speak

© 2003, 2004 Sweet Home Press

Table of Contents continued

Supplemental Materials

S-01a.	Conversation Starter Cards
S-01b	Getting to Know Each Other
S-03a	I.O.U.s
S-03b	Out Ouch
S-05	Don't Need to Say Everything Poster
S-10	Match Expressions to Body Language
S-11	George Washington's Rules of Civility
S-14	Sabotage!
S-15	Please
S-21	Stop, Look and Listen
S-M	Memorization

Conversation with Character

Introduction

Conversation is becoming a lost art in today's culture. Families sit side-by-side watching television, teenagers can do little more than "grunt" and spouses quickly share pertinent information before falling off to an exhausted sleep. Yet relationships are, most would agree, what life is all about. And conversation is the primary tool we are given to develop those relationships past the level of business partnerships, past superficial banalities and into the deep and beautiful sharing of lives for which we long.

Our goal as Christian parents is to help our children learn to relate to people as Jesus did. We want them to have the mind of Christ and see people as He does. We want them to have his heart for the unlovely, the socially inept, and the lonely, as well as for friends and family. Studying the scriptures together helps us see how Jesus spoke to lepers, to sinners, and to His Father.

The Golden Rule sums up the type of conversation we desire for our families. Listen the way you want to be listened to. Talk about others and to others the way you want them to talk about/to you. Consider ways to bless your conversational partner, rather than focus solely on your own interests.

As with most things, exercising good conversation skills comes down to a matter of the heart. It is our hope that this book will help you work with your child to weed out bad habits that hinder loving communication and to cultivate those good habits that make it easier for excellent fruit to grow.

Words are powerful. They can tear down or build up. They can destroy relationships or deepen them. Wisely chosen words can bring us satisfaction while foolish ones can bring years of regret. How important it is, then, for us as parents to train our children in their

Meet *Character*

Hello! My name is "Character."

Sweet Home Press recruited me to encourage you and your children toward conversation with good character. We will be seeing each other along the way.

It is my hope, and certainly the hope and prayer of everyone at *Sweet Home Press*, that your children will be like shining stars that "appear as lights in the world." (Philippians 2:15)

Conversation with Character

> **Proverbs 12:14**
>
> A man will be satisfied with good by the fruit of his words...

> **Ideal conversation**
>
> should be a matter of equal give and take, but too often it is all "take."

proper use! May the Lord richly bless your efforts as you help your children learn and practice the art of effective communication.

How to Use this Book

This book supplies organized, bite-sized concepts, easily taught. Simply reading the lesson to children will not, however, change their communication habits. Like playing an instrument or cooking, knowledge comes first, but PRACTICE makes perfect! That is why we include one or more activities with each lesson.

Adapt the lessons to your teaching style and to the learning style of your children. Our suggestions, however, are:

- Tackle no more than one lesson per week. Take two weeks on lessons needing extra attention in your home.

- Practice the current week's skill at the dinner table and in other family discussions.

- Play **brief** rounds of the "Ahh" and "Uh-oh" game. (see right column on next page). Do it with humor and grace. Keep the focus on love.

- Each lesson includes a Bible verse. Have your children memorize the verse to reinforce the lesson.

    Note: To add to your child's reservoir of wisdom (from which conversation is enriched), use *Quotes with Character*, also available from Sweet Home Press.

- Before a family visit, review skills taught in the lessons and discuss how they might be applied in the upcoming situation.

Notes added for your information, only, are preceded with "Parents:" and often appear in [brackets].

© 2003-2004 Sweet Home Press

A Few Supplies

You will find the following supplies helpful for the activities in some lessons:

- A ball
- Drawing paper
- Pencils, crayons or colored pencils
- Scissors
- Large safety pins—one for each family member
- Notebook or section of notebook

All other supplies needed are provided in the back of the book in the *Supplemental Materials* section.

Conversation with Character

The "Uh-oh" and "Ah" Game

Watch it , now!

The flock of one American church culture gives the preacher instant, ongoing sermon feedback with frequent interjections like "Amen," "Preach it," and "Watch it, now!"

When your family practices good conversation, try giving feedback. You might use a simple "Ahh," when someone demonstrates good conversation skills and "Uh-oh," when the opposite is true. Or select your own signals.

You will be amazed at what good listeners children become, and how quickly lessons are put into practice.

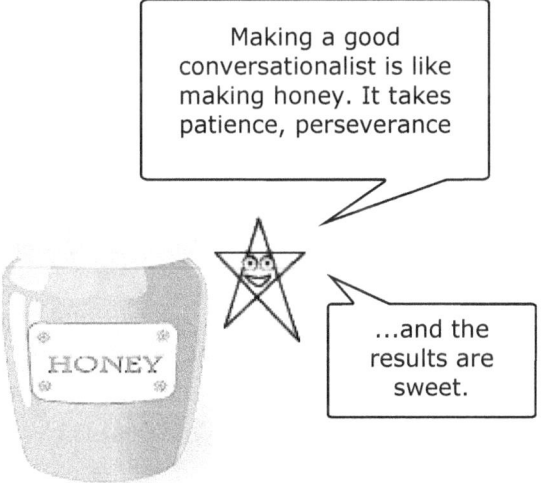

Making a good conversationalist is like making honey. It takes patience, perseverance

...and the results are sweet.

A Note about Our Writing Style

As you read appropriate sections of this book to your children, you may find the writing style and vocabulary above a younger person's grasp. We believe in presenting children a standard to which they can aspire. As a parent, it gives you an opportunity to be the expert, interpreting and explaining words and phrases children don't understand.

1 Start a Conversation

Philippians 2:4
Do not merely look out for your own personal interests, but also for the interests of others.

Lingering Impressions
First impressions linger, either like rose petals or like last week's fish.

— Anonymous

"It is commonly observed that, when two Englishmen meet, their first talk is of the weather; they are in haste to tell each other what each must already know, that it is hot or cold, bright or cloudy, windy or calm." - Samuel Johnson

Pity the poor fellow who can think of no better conversation starter than the weather. This lesson helps transform you from weatherman to fisherman.

Learn How to Fish For Conversation

A good fisherman tries various types of bait until he finds one that works in his present situation. The same can be true for a person trying to strike up a conversation. If your first few questions or suggested topics don't get much response, try a few more until you get a "bite."

It is often helpful to think through possible conversation starters ahead of time rather than trying to come up with ideas when face to face.

Avoid questions that can be answered "yes" or "no." [Parent: Ask children why. Discuss.]

Remember that people like to talk about themselves and their own interests and experiences.

"I will make you fishers of men..."

© 2003, 2004 Sweet Home Press

Conversation with Character

Here are some sample conversation starters:

- ? If you could take a family vacation any place in the world, where would you go?
- ? If you could have any animal as a pet, which would you choose?
- ? What…(movie, sport, activity, color, book, etc.) do you like? Tell me why?
- ? What is something that you do well?
- ? What family traditions do you especially like?
- ? What do you like best about (a hobby or interest)?
- ? How did you meet my parents?
- ? Tell me about your family.
- ? What do you like best about your job? Or being a mom?
- ? Are you from around here? If not, where are you from?

Suggested Activity

See **Supplemental Materials S-01a and S-01b** for the activities that go with this lesson.

[Parent: When you are on the way to visit someone this week, consider discussing appropriate conversation starters for the person(s) you will visit.]

Practice basic greetings with any children who have not yet learned. These might include: "Hello, How are you today?" or "I'm pleased to meet you sir/ma'am." Try them on each other to make sure these words are comfortable for everyone.

Parent: Avoid Bad Starts

Here are some real-life examples of bad conversation starters you can help your younger child(ren) avoid:

Calling attention to how people look, talk or act.
- *"What's that thing on your face?"*
- *"You talk funny."*

Calling attention to an obvious problem with the other person.
- *"What's that funny smell; is that you?!"* Or
- *"Why did your mother have to talk to you?" "What did you do wrong?" "Did it hurt?"*

Making a cultural error.
- *"How old are you?"* (to an adult) Or
- *"How much money do you make?"*

If you've been a parent long, then you can probably add some to the list. The point is, parents can't assume a child knows not to say these things. Training early is time well spent.

© 2003, 2004 Sweet Home Press

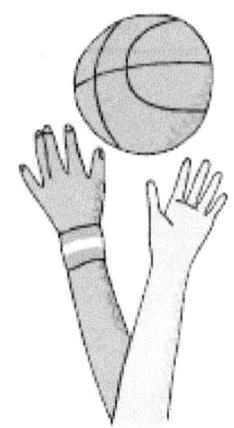

2 Pass the Ball

Do you ever watch animals playing with a ball or other object? Our two dogs don't pass a ball or a stick to each other. The prized object is taken only by force.

As people, we are able to teach pets certain behaviors that are contrary to their nature. Unfortunately, just because we are humans does not mean we naturally share things (like turns in conversation). We, too, must be taught and trained.

This lesson teaches passing the conversational ball to others.

Pass the Ball to Others

Whether your weakness is rambling, repeating or talking about yourself too much, the quickest way to correct the problem is to let someone else talk for awhile.

This is not to say that everyone should be quiet all the time, lest all conversations cease. However, according to the book of James, we should devote more time to listening and less to talking.

What if others in a conversation don't seem to have much to say? Note that the title of this lesson is not "Drop the Ball." It is "Pass the Ball." That is what you do to take the focus off of yourself and yet keep a good conversation going.

Still don't get it? We pass the conversation ball by asking someone a question. Think of a question related to the current topic of conversation. If the topic is food, a good

---

Luke 6:31

Treat others the same way you want them to treat you.

Let Go

It is all right to hold a conversation but you should let go of it now and then.

- Richard Armour

© 2003, 2004 Sweet Home Press

Conversation with Character

ball-passing question might be "What kind of foods do you especially like?" or "Do you like to cook (if so, then what)?"

No one can long resist the invitation to tell their ideas, experiences, opinions and desires. Passing the ball not only improves the conversation, it shows kindness and respect to others, and it grows friendship.

Hopefully, your friend will eventually pass the ball back. Be patient and attentive until they do. In a good conversation, all participants question and everyone gets to talk.

Suggested Activity

[Parent: Holding a ball, announce that you are going to play a new game. Stand looking at the ball and holding it. Toss it up and down and play with it a bit. Act excited and animated about the ball—telling what a nice ball it is and how much you enjoy holding it. Then, enthusiastically say, "Isn't this new game FUN?!" When the inevitable "NO" resounds, explain that this is what it is like when one person "holds the ball" in a conversation—not much fun.]

Now play a game of catch, or roll the ball back and forth to each other on the floor. That's a lot more fun for everyone, isn't it?

Then have a conversation. The person speaking holds the ball. When the speaker asks someone else a question, they pass the ball to the next speaker. Can't think of a conversation topic? Try the suggestions in the right column.*

[Parent: If someone goes on too long without passing the ball, point it out and tell them it is time to pass the ball by asking someone a question. Using an actual ball is optional, but may be helpful initially to reinforce the concept.]

"Score" an Assist

According to the official statistician's manual for college basketball, "A player is credited with an 'assist' when the player makes, in the judgment of the statistician, the principal pass contributing directly to a field goal." In other words, when you pass the ball so someone else can score, you've done a very good thing!

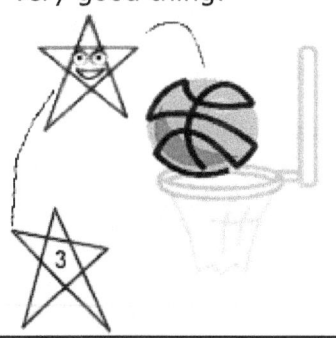

*Topic Suggestions

Can't think of a topic for the activity? Try these:
- "Where should we go on vacation?"
- "If our family had a favorite book (other than the Bible), what would it be?"
- Describe your parent's room.

© 2003, 2004 Sweet Home Press

3 Keep an "I" Out

Proverbs 18:2

A fool does not delight in understanding,
But only in revealing his own mind.

Proverbs 27:2

Let another praise you, and not your own mouth;
A stranger, and not your own lips.

Me, Me, Me, Me...

If you your ears would save from jeers,
These things keep meekly hid:
Myself and I, and mine and my,
And how I do and did.

- Unknown

One of our daughters likes to tell us about the dream she had the night before. She has learned an appropriate way to earn the opportunity, by first asking, "Did anyone have any dreams last night?" Some say "Yes" and tell about their dream. Others respond "No" or "I don't recall."

Only after each person has had an opportunity to tell about their dream does she tell about her own. She is careful to "keep an I out," letting others first have their say.

This lesson shows how to keep the focus off of self.

Don't Focus on Yourself

Don't talk about yourself, unless specifically asked. "I, I, I" conversations are BORING to others. Have you ever been with a person who habitually returns the focus to themself, no matter what is said?

Such conversations go something like this:

> George: *"Isn't this a lovely day?"*
>
> Fred: *"Yes, but my arthritis is acting up. It always gets bad on days with even a little humidity. How're you feeling?"*
>
> George: *"Well, I'm still having some problems with that arm I fractured months ago."*
>
> Fred: *"Join the club. My ear has really been hurting lately. Why just the other day it hurt so badly I didn't think I could stand it."*
>
> George: *"Oh, I'm really sorry to hear*

© 2003, 2004 Sweet Home Press

that. May I show you what I bought my sister for her birthday? I'm so excited—I think she will really like it!"

Fred: "Isn't that nice? I had one of those when I was younger, except bigger..."

And so it goes...with the focus always on the great "I." Whatever the other person says, Fred thinks of something about himself that he just must tell.

You may have many admirable qualities and great accomplishments, but others should rarely learn that from you. Let them observe your actions or hear it from someone else. Sure, you want to share news of your success with those closest to you, but do so with humility: For example, "I was so surprised when I won the writing contest!"

In all your conversation, keep an eye out for "I." Each time you shift the conversation to yourself, think of it as handing out an I.O.U.

I.O.U. normally means "I owe you" something. It can also mean "I over you," or "I am more important than you."

When you talk about yourself, think of it as handing out an I.O.U. Now you owe the next person a turn to talk.

Suggested Activity

Parent: Cut out the "I.O.U." slips in **Supplemental Materials S-03a** and give each person a stack to keep in their pocket for a day (or clipped or pinned to clothing). When someone hears someone talk about themselves, take an I.O.U. from them. See who has the most and least I.O.U.s at the end of the day.

Try it a second day to see who learned from the first day's activity.

Picture It

As an alternate or additional activity, draw a picture to illustrate this lesson. Here are some ideas:

- Someone who says "I" and "me" a lot, like an opera singer singing "Mi, mi, mi, mi," with an audience that has fallen asleep.
- Color the I.O.U.'s to go with the main activity.
- Turn the letters in the words "I" and "you" into people. "I" people dress badly. "You" people dress attractively.

Out-Ouching

"Out-ouching" is topping someone else's story of trouble by telling your own tale of woe. Read the article about this annoying habit in **Supplemental Materials S-03b**.

4 Show Interest and Effort

I suppose our cat is like most others. If you have a cat, then this will sound familiar. Our cat does no tricks, won't come when we call him, and he ignores us when we scold for getting into mischief. He takes little interest and exerts no effort to do the things we want him to do.

Oh, but if it is his idea—something he wants—well, that's a different story. If he wants food, he will watch our every motion and run toward the feeding bowl at any sign of our obedience to his desires.

If we sleep late, the cat will jump up on the bed and stick his nose in our face to see if we are still asleep (when we should be up feeding him). He is totally disinterested when we want something, but a model of interest and effort when it suits him.

This lesson explains how interest and effort contribute to a good conversation.

Showing Interest Takes Effort

LISTEN, LISTEN, LISTEN! Listening is probably the most important part of being a good conversationalist! Listen with your ears and with your mind. Your curiosity about what the other person is saying fuels good conversation.

Have you been in a conversation and noticed that someone is not really listening, but rather waiting for a pause so they can jump in with what they want to say? This attitude turns a conversation into a series of monologues (long speeches made by one

---

Proverbs 1:8-9

Hear, my son, your father's instruction
And do not forsake your mother's teaching;
Indeed, they are a graceful wreath to your head
And ornaments about your neck.

Listening = Learning

Learning is a result of listening, which in turn leads to even better listening and attentiveness to the other person.

- Alice Miller

Conversation with Character

person, often monopolizing a conversation). Monologues make real communication impossible.

You need to pay attention to everything that everyone says in a conversation, even if you don't think it has anything to do with you. Someone may suddenly ask you to comment or give your opinion. It is inconsiderate if you must keep asking what was said.

Do you know someone who often answers "What?" when spoken to? It could be that those around them don't speak clearly. Or it may be that they don't listen well. Listening is an active state requiring work on your part...even cats have learned that much.
(Parent: Ask your child(ren) to recap the points made about listening, to see if they were listening!)

Suggested Activity

What questions might you ask to show interest and to further the conversation, after you hear the following statements?

"I deliver newspapers."

[Parent: Answers will vary. Examples might be: How long have you been doing that? Do you enjoy it? What do you do with the money you earn?]

"On Thursday I went to play rehearsal."

[Parent: What play are you doing? When will it be performed? What part do you play? Is this your first play?]

"I got a dog for my birthday."

[Parent: How exciting! What kind is it? What did you name it? Is it male or female? How big will it get? What do you feed it?]

Now, take turns making a brief statement and have others ask questions about what was said. See how long you can keep going on one topic. Before you know it, you'll have a conversation!

Listening Actively

Some ways to practice active listening are:

- Repeat in your head everything the other person says.
- Say it back to them OCCASIONALLY in your own words: "So what you are saying is…"
- Ask questions about what was said.
- Keep eye contact and be sure your body posture is turned towards others to let them know that you truly are listening.

Batter Up

The best professional baseball players have learned how to keep their eyes "glued" to the ball.

The best conversationalists keep themselves glued to the conversation.

© 2003, 2004 Sweet Home Press

5 Don't Interrupt

(Parent: See suggested activity #1 to start the lesson)

Dale Carnegie, born in 1888, was a writer, teacher, salesman and regular on the radio. He was most famous for his classic book, How to Win Friends and Influence People, in which he said:

> "If you want to know how to make people shun you and laugh at you behind your back and even despise you, here is the recipe. Never listen to anyone for long. Talk incessantly about yourself. If you have an idea while the other fellow is talking, don't wait for him to finish. He isn't so smart as you. Why waste your time listening to his idle chatter? Bust right in and interrupt him in the middle of a sentence."

This lesson helps interrupt discourteous interruption.

Wait Your Turn

Interrupting others stems from self-centeredness—our desire to be heard, recognized, seen as important and knowledgeable. A habit of interrupting is the quick path to being disliked, and is one of the greatest obstacles to good conversation.

The best antidote for the interruption habit, aside from simply keeping quiet, is listening with all your might, as discussed in the lesson *Show Interest and Effort*.

Concentrate on what the other person is saying. Let the spotlight fall on that person

---

James 1:19

...But everyone must be quick to hear, slow to speak...

Interrupt...Later

If you must interrupt me, then please wait until I am finished!

- Anonymous

while you practice patience. Wait for a pause when no one else is talking. To make sure you don't interrupt, allow about two seconds after each person is done before starting to talk.

One family we know has a signal they use at home. When someone wants to make a comment, they hold up a finger. Other family members take note of the finger and make sure that person has a chance to speak at the next reasonable opportunity. Since the person now knows they will not miss a chance to comment, they can relax and listen while waiting patiently for others to finish speaking.

If interruptions do occur, say "excuse me" and allow the other person to finish. Never take the words out of someone's mouth by finishing a sentence for them.

Suggested Activity

[Parent: Ask a child to recite something familiar—a song, poem, or nursery rhyme. Interrupt as often as possible in a friendly manner. At the end, discuss how annoying that was. Ex: Jack and Jill (I always liked the name Jill) went up the hill (I wonder where that hill was?) etc.]

[Parent: Here is a week-long activity. Mom or Dad should have a noise-maker of some kind readily available at mealtimes and family conversation times. Whenever someone interrupts, make that noise so that family members become more aware of bad habits. If no noise-maker is available, a verbal "beeeep!" will do.]

Note: Another device for giving feedback to both good and bad conversational habits is the "Ahh" and "Uh-oh" game, explained in the *Introduction* section of this book.

Conversation with Character

Pick Up Where You Left Off

Some interruptions cannot be avoided—like when Mom says it is suppertime or when the waiter asks (again) if you want more water.

The next opportunity you have to talk with that person, try to recall what they were saying. Pick up the conversation where they left off: "Now, what were you saying about...," or, "I'd like to hear more about..."

That reassures the other person that what they had to say is important to you.

Hold that Thought

Interruptions come when people just must say whatever they are thinking.

See the poster in **Supplemental Materials S-05**.

© 2003, 2004 Sweet Home Press

6 Speak Blessings

Words that bless and words that curse were often spoken in the Bible, and things happened as a result.

Jesus said, "You are forgiven," and what he said matters for eternity.

People make agreements, and their reputation rests on whether they keep their word.

Words mean something. Why not use the opportunity to speak as an opportunity to bless others with your words? Romans 12:13 says we should bless even those who persecute us. If we can bless those who persecute us, how much easier it should be to bless those with whom we just happen to be in conversation.

Speak from A Storehouse of Blessings

How can we speak words that bless unless we know such words?

It is a blessing to speak truth. Indeed, it is a blessing to speak God's Word, because God's Word is powerful. The Bible says the Word is sharper than a two-edged sword. For example, "Margaret, you are so talented. As the Bible says, we are 'His workmanship, created in Christ Jesus for good works.' That's what I see in you."

Numbers 6:22-27

Then the LORD spoke to Moses, saying, "Speak to Aaron and to his sons, saying, 'Thus you shall bless the sons of Israel. You shall say to them:

The LORD bless you, and keep you;

The LORD make His face shine on you,

And be gracious to you;

The LORD lift up His countenance on you,

And give you peace.'

"So they shall invoke My name on the sons of Israel, and I then will bless them."

To the Moon!

I see the moon,
And the moon sees me;
God bless the moon,
And God bless me.

- Unknown

© 2003, 2004 Sweet Home Press

It is also a blessing to affirm Godly qualities in another person: "Joe, you are such a trustworthy man. I appreciate that about you."

The opposite of a blessing is a curse. Calling someone a dummy is a curse. Call someone a dummy often and, eventually, they may start acting that way. Words have power.

Words of wisdom, said in the right place and at the right time, are very good gifts. They are words of blessing also. Since children have had few years to gain wisdom and words of blessing, it is useful to have some mentally tucked away.

Suggested Activity

[Parent: Have your child copy a quote each day into a notebook and memorize it .(This activity doubles as handwriting practice). He or she can recite the quote at the dinner table and make it a topic of conversation.

These quotes become part of your child's stored up words of blessings, ready to use in conversation with others. Encourage them to speak these blessings to others and give them positive feedback when they do.

In addition to blessing others, wise words become powerful, life-long blessings and encouragement to your child. Your child's head will be filled with *something*. Why not make it the best?]

Conversation with Character

Words of Blessing

"Many hands make light work." -John Heywood

"God loves each of us as if there was only one of us." -Augustine

"Well begun is half done." -Aristotle

"One thing people always appreciate is being appreciated." –Unknown

"No man is poor who has a godly mother." -Abraham Lincoln

"I have not failed. I've just found 10,000 ways that won't work." -Thomas Edison

"There's no place like home." -(said by many)

The Bible is a great source for quotes. In addition, the

<u>Quotes with Character</u>

book is designed to help you make this a year-long activity, containing 201 quotes of wisdom from men and women throughout history. Available from Sweet Home Press at **sweethomepress.com**

© 2003, 2004 Sweet Home Press

7 Be Concise

I was barely engaged in conversation with a Russian woman who had just returned to Moscow from a visit to England. While in England, she discovered she has an extraordinary gift for learning languages. This native Russian speaker obviously learned English at an astonishing pace, as she demonstrated to me that day.

Her English guests, it seemed, taught her one particularly telling phrase. "I'm a chatter-box!" she proclaimed, with a smile.

How wonderful to learn new languages. May we learn to tame our use of the first language before embarking on world domination. Learn here how to make the best use of few words.

Keep Comments Brief and to the Point

All of us have been in a conversations that seemed to go on (and on) without our participation, save an occasional nod or one syllable reply. These situations often leave us feeling the other person values us as little more than an *audience*.

Jesus says to treat others the way we would like to be treated. One way we can do that is by keeping our comments brief and to the point.

Make short, appropriate comments that relate to the discussion topic, but don't belabor the point. Offering too much detail seldom interests anyone but you.

Proverbs 10:19

When words are many, sin is not absent, but he who holds his tongue is wise.

Less is More

If I am to speak ten minutes, I need a week for preparation; if fifteen minutes, three days; if half an hour, two days; if an hour, I am ready now.

-Woodrow Wilson

© 2003, 2004 Sweet Home Press

It's better to leave people wanting to know more—to have them ask for more detail—than to offer more than is desired.

Avoid long stories that leave no chance for the other person to comment. Don't be a chatterbox!

Suggested Activity

Read the following words said on the telephone. Decide what the main thought is. See how few words you can use to say what really needs to be said. The paragraph now has 162 words. How many words are left after you shorten it?

Two days ago at five o'clock, when we usually set the table, a man came to the back door—or was it the side door because that is the door the cat usually goes out—I know now, it was the front door. The man wanted to wash our windows for pay, the way my big brother used to do in the summers to make money to buy a car. He actually ended up getting an old red Ford truck and I got to ride in the back on the fourth of July to go see the fireworks. Anyway, Dad said he could wash the windows and the man's ladder slipped and broke the upstairs window in my sister's room next to her bed. That is why Dad asked me to call you, Uncle Harry, and see if you can come replace the window for us, since you are in the glass business and would probably like to do something like that.

Yawn

If you happen to recall the song called "The Song that Never Ends," (theme song for the Shari Lewis puppet show, *Lamb Chop*) sing it together as a fun additional activity. For those who don't know the song, it truly is a song that never ends, until someone finally puts a stop to it. (You might use another song that makes the same point.)

Conversation with Character

The Laconic Calvin Coolidge

The laconic Calvin Coolidge (nicknamed "Silent Cal"), spoke so little that a dinner guest boasted that she could elicit more than two words from him.

He replied "You lose."

Add the word **laconic** to your vocabulary: **(sounds like lay-kon-ick)**

It means "concise, using few words." Laconic is from the Greek *Lakon*, who was a Spartan known for brief speech. Use laconic in a sentence now and try to incorporate it in your conversation this week.

The Song that Never Ends

This is the song that never ends.
It just goes on and on my friend.
Some people started singing it, not knowing what it was,
And they'll continue singing it forever, just because
(repeat as long as you dare)

© 2003, 2004 Sweet Home Press

*I've heard this **how** many times...?*

8 Say It Just Once

Do you find yourself inwardly cringing each time you pass a certain building, because you know exactly what someone will say, like "That's the building where I took ballet lessons?" Worse, have you watched someone's eyes glaze over as you launch into a story, only to realize that you told them that story already...yesterday?

This lesson teaches how to avoid the error of repeating tales and over-elaborating.

Don't Repeat

Don't repeat yourself, either by telling the same story again or by going back over details that seemed to especially interest or amuse people the first time through.

Small children and older people are sometimes predictable. If they see a certain building, or object, or hear a certain word or name that reminds them of an old story, they will retell it in much the same way. We should exercise patience and love with the immaturity of children and the need for older people to reminisce (sometimes under the handicap of forgetfulness), but make sure you aren't the one who retells stories.

Repetition can sometimes induce deliberate humor.

In our home, when the word "shrimp" is mentioned, we can count on Daddy to retell his shrimp joke.: "It never bothered me, being short until I went into a seafood restaurant one day and asked the waiter 'Do you serve shrimp here?' and he said 'Sure,

---

Proverbs 17:28

Even a fool,
when he keeps silent,
is considered wise...

Too Much Is Too Much

Many things are of interest when briefly told and for the first time; nothing interests when too long dwelt upon; little interests that is told a second time.

- Emily Post

© 2003, 2004 Sweet Home Press

Conversation with Character

sit down, buddy, we'll serve anyone!"
The retelling, and not the story, is the source of humor—but you can seldom count on having such a receptive audience.

Most of us must take care that our repeated stories do not become the *unintentional* object of snickering.

Repeated phrases and sentences can also be used as a substitute for direct communication. How many times in your house has someone mentioned three times that the ketchup is almost empty, rather than offering to go to the refrigerator or pantry for more?

[Parent: Ask child to summarize the lesson.]

Suggested Activity

[Parent: Tell the following story as a fun way to reinforce the idea. Continue until the point is clear and/or the groans drown you out!]

It was a dark and stormy night, and all the boys were gathered around the campfire. And one of them said, "Captain, tell us a story." The captain said, "All right..."

"t was a dark and stormy night and all the boys were gathered around the campfire. And one of them said, "Captain, tell us a story." The captain said, "All right..."

[Parent: Remember to practice each lesson throughout the week—in the car, at mealtimes, etc. I guess some things ARE worth repeating.]

It was a dark and stormy night and all the boys were gathered around the campfire. And one of them said, "Captain, tell us a story." The captain said, "All right..."

It was a dark and stormy night and all the boys were gathered around the campfire. and one of them said , 'Captain, tell us a story.' And the Captain said, All right...

Distracting Words and Phrases

Another distraction from an otherwise good conversation is repeated use of certain vague words or phrases. Current examples in American culture are "like," "really" and "you know." For example:

"*Like* we *really* just wanted to *like, you know*, go to the concert." At best, this sentence is not concise, but repeating these vague words throughout a conversation detracts from effective communication.

Other distractions may be frequent interjections, like "and, uh." Another might be overuse of faddish adjectives like "cool," "freaky" or "bad" (meaning "good"), etc.

What other words and phrases do you hear that get in the way of a good conversation?

Which distracting words and phrases do you need to limit in your conversation?

9 Make Smooth Transitions

If you have ever gotten into a pool of cold water on a hot day, then you know how a not-so-smooth transition feels. There are no smooth transitions between hot and cold. You have two choices: Either jump right in (giving your whole body a sudden jolt) or ease in slowly. Some people like the "ease in slowly" method. They say it makes a smoother transition from hot to cold.

Most conversation topics are neither hot nor cold, but transition from one topic to another can give people a sudden and unpleasant jolt. This lesson helps you make smooth transitions between topics.

Easy Does It

Change topics only when it seems everyone has had their say and is ready to move on. When you change the subject too quickly, some people feel left out or not really heard.

If a friend has just told you that her grandmother died and how sad that makes her feel, this is not the right time to suddenly tell about your birthday party. Your friend needs to know you heard her and feel sympathy for her. You need to wait until you are sure she is ready to go on to another topic before you bring up the party. Maybe your birthday party should wait for another day.

Try to remain attentive to a conversation that doesn't interest you, or about which there is little else of importance to say. Wait

---

Ecclesiastes 3:1

There is an appointed time for everything...

When You Have Had Enough

There are times when I think that the ideal library is composed solely of reference books. They are like understanding friends—always ready to meet your mood, always ready to change the subject when you have had enough of this or that.

- J. Donald Adams

© 2003, 2004 Sweet Home Press

for the right moment to change the subject.

Knowing when to change the subject is an art that takes practice, good listening skills and wisdom.

The most graceful way to change subjects is by making a smooth transition. To a friend who just told about a trip to the mountains, you might ask about the highest mountain they have seen, and that might lead in to a mutual interest in geography.

Consider also how you might transition into a topic that very much interests the other person, or that gives them the opportunity to express their feelings or opinions.

No matter the two topics, making a smooth transition from one to the other shows your maturity and sensitivity to others.

First, allow each person a chance to comment on the current topic. Then make the transition to a different topic.

Suggested Activity

Practice conversational transitions. Have one person tell about an experience they had. Have another person find the right time to and ways to transition to another topic. Try these, or make up your own:

First topic: The last visit to relatives.

Transition to: A favorite food.

First topic: An interesting craft project.

Transition to: A recent math lesson.

Optional Challenge: Think of the two most opposite topics you can, and try to make transitions that get you from one topic to the other. You might want to set a time limit.

Conversation with Character

Changing Topics without Warning

Some people, whether because of an active or a wandering mind, forget to let others know they have changed subjects. Listen to how one person keeps changing the subject without warning.

Wasn't it great seeing the Barnes family again?

Yes, it has been a long time.

I wonder where she got it.

Got what?

Why, that beautiful tablecloth, of course.

Well, I imagine she got it on her trip.

Nine times I asked for the recipe, but...

What recipe?

The chocolate cake recipe.

Oh, that...

Did you get two or three?

I assure you, I only ate one piece of cake!

No, I mean when we stopped at the store on the way home. Did you buy two bottles or three? Aren't you listening?

© 2003, 2004 Sweet Home Press

10 Control Body Language

Proverbs 16:30

He who winks his eyes does so to devise perverse things;

He who compresses his lips brings evil to pass.

Full of Secrets

(The body is) a marvelous machine...a chemical laboratory, a power-house. Every movement, voluntary or involuntary, full of secrets and marvels!

- Theodor Herz

Volumes have been written on body language and scholars have made careers deciding what all of our body actions and postures mean. It has been suggested that 70% of what we communicate comes not through our words, but through our body language.

This lesson helps you identify and control your body language.

Make Sure Your Body Says What You Mean

Body language includes your posture, the expression on your face and all the motions you make during conversation. It may also include the distance you keep between yourself and others.

Hand and face motions contribute heavily to communication. Yet, such motions and posture come so naturally that you may be telling people much more than you think.

Some body language is cultural. We learn it from the people we live around, from TV, from magazines, etc.

Some motions mean different things in different cultures! Did you know, for example, that a Sri Lankan moves his head from side to side for "Yes" and nods the head up and down for "No?"

Some Middle Eastern cultures regard it very rude to show the bottom of your shoe. Many East Asians bow to show respect. A Romanian is likely to stand close to you as he

© 2003, 2004 Sweet Home Press

Conversation with Character

speaks, while an Englishman may keep his distance and avoid body contact.

Other body language is universal. A smile means the same in the United States as in Zimbabwe. If you see someone sitting at a desk with their head cradled in their hands, you conclude that they are either tired, ill or distressed. Such body language is the same for everyone.

When you practice good conversation skills, you use your motions and posture to convey interest in what others say and to enhance your own communication. Use body language to show respect for others and that they have your full attention.

Suggested Activities

See the activity in Supplemental Materials S-10.

While much body language comes naturally, we can also use exaggerated facial expressions and gestures to communicate beyond words. If you and another person speak different languages, how can you both be friendly and communicate without words? The following activity is a bit like *charades*.

Using gestures and facial expressions, one person asks a question, without speaking. The other person answers, without speaking. Here are the questions. [Parent: Tell the question to only one child, so the other must guess at what is being asked.]

- Would you like a drink?
- May I sit down?
- Where can I eat chicken?
- How much does that book cost?
- Will it rain?
- May I cut your hair?

Show Interest

To show interest and respect during conversation,

- Keep your body relaxed and attentive.
- Lean slightly toward the speaker.
- Nod occasionally for encouragement.
- Pleasantly smile, unless the topic is very serious.
- Make frequent eye contact with the speaker, but don't just stare.
- Avoid yawning, fidgeting, and looking away. Such actions communicate a lack of interest.

Irritating Mannerisms

See the lesson *Overcoming Irritating Mannerisms* for more instruction on body language.

© 2003, 2004 Sweet Home Press

Proverbs 6:12-13

A worthless person, a wicked man,

Is the one who walks with a perverse mouth,

Who winks with his eyes, who signals with his feet,

Who points with his fingers.

Roll Not the Eyes

Shake not the head, feet, or legs; roll not the eyes; lift not one eyebrow higher than the other, wry not the mouth, and bedew no man's face with your spittle...

- George Washington's *Rules of Civility and Decent Behavior in Company and Conversation* (Find excerpts from Washington's list in **Supplemental Materials S-11**.)

11 Overcome Irritating Mannerisms

I have a bad habit that is a life-long struggle. Too often, I don't look into a person's eyes when I speak. Had I worked on breaking this habit when I was young, it would probably not have followed me well into adulthood.

I believe this habit has kept me from getting certain jobs that require good face-to-face conversation skills. I would be more convincing and seem more sincere. People would find my words more interesting.

In chapter 8, *Say It Just Once*, we reviewed in the right column words and phrases that can become irritating to the listener when overused. Lesson 11 examines physical mannerisms and speech habits that detract from a good conversation—habits worth tackling early in life.

Break Bad Habits

Physical mannerisms not only annoy others, they make it very difficult for others to follow a conversation. Examples are cracking knuckles, drumming fingers on the table, chewing gum, rubbing your nose (or worse) and playing with your hair.

Control facial expressions that convey disapproval or annoyance before others have fully expressed themselves. A scowl causes others to lose concentration or give up trying to explain, and it takes attention away from the speaker and onto yourself.

You may not recognize your own habits.

© 2003, 2004 Sweet Home Press

Conversation with Character

After all, you don't face yourself when you speak. Ask someone close to you if you have irritating or distracting mannerisms.

Let your normal voice be low and pleasant. Speaking always with a high pitch might communicate excitement when not intended. Speaking ever in low monotone says "I am bored with this conversation."

Let your words be clear and distinct. Don't say "Didjagetcherring" when "Did you get your ring?" can be said with good effort.

Some distracting physical habits are lifelong struggles. People who stutter or who have physical or emotional handicaps need plenty of help and encouragement. Many habits, however, can be overcome in a week or a few months. By recognizing bad habits and making a conscious effort, you can overcome them before they overcome you and smother good conversation.

Suggested Activity

Use a video camera to record a conversation between family members. Select topics that suit your family. Watch the recording to see what areas need work in both body language and irritating mannerisms.
[Parent: If you don't have a video camera, then take notes so you can report later what you observed.]

Do you see or hear bad habits? Write on a piece of paper what you should work on. Make it your goal to stay aware of your own bad habits, and make a deliberate effort to overcome. Repeat as needed. In between recordings, practice on your own by speaking into a large mirror.

Read short stories onto tape for younger siblings, friends or for children at a homeless shelter or hospital. Work on improving voice quality and clarity.

Listen Past the Bad Habits

As a listener, you can serve others and help save a conversation by overlooking bad habits.

Make it your special challenge to listen past other people's bad habits and attentively hear and understand what is said. The other person will appreciate your efforts. You may be the only person willing to engage in a conversation with them today.

Parents have a responsibility to lovingly point out bad habits and encourage a child to overcome. Children have a different role. It is a child's important job with friends or siblings to listen past their bad habits, unless instructed otherwise by a parent.

Hey, Saturn, did you get your ring?

© 2003, 2004 Sweet Home Press

12 Don't Slam Doors

Ephesians 4:2-3

...showing tolerance for one another in love, being diligent to preserve the unity of the Spirit in the bond of peace.

Wisdom's Doors

The doors of wisdom are never shut.

-Benjamin Franklin

One of the first things children learn after beginning to walk is *don't slam doors.* Slamming doors is an annoying habit that is inconsiderate of others in the house.

When I was a small boy, my older sister had a way of ending a conversation with me by going to her bedroom and slamming the door. I can't say that I blame her, considering what a little pest I was. We were both at fault.

Sometimes we slam the door on conversation. Even well-mannered adults at times slam a conversation door shut without meaning to. This lesson helps you recognize and avoid conversational door slamming.

Keep the Conversation from Slamming Shut

A good conversation takes work on EVERYONE's part. If you only grunt or say "yes" or "no" or make flat contradictory statements, you make real communication impossible. Suppose you ask a friend these questions, and suppose they answer like this:

Question: "What kind of songs do you like?"

Answer: "None. "

Question: "Which team are you for in the big game this week?"

Answer: "Who cares?"

© 2003, 2004 Sweet Home Press

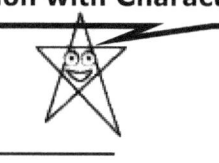

Conversation with Character

Now, would you feel like a door was slammed on your conversation? How about the following statements and responses?

Statement: "My aunt is very sick in the hospital."

Response: "I visited the hospital once."

Statement: "I'm so excited. We are getting a puppy!"

Response: "Dogs make such messes."

Responses like these make it seem like the other person is not interested in what interests you, and that they don't care about your feelings.

When has this happened to you? [Parent: Pause for answers.]

Now, think about it, have you ever answered someone in a way that slams the door on them? [Parent: Pause for answers. Encourage honesty.]

Suggested Activity

Go back over each of the questions and statements above. Try giving a reply that would keep a good conversation going, making sure to "throw the ball" back after you answer, as discussed in the lesson *Pass the Ball*.

Make a poster with the words "Don't be a Door Slammer" and hang it on a door as a reminder this week. Add appropriate decorations or illustrations to the poster.

Re-Opening Closed Doors

Some people make it hard to have a conversation. Maybe they have been hurt many times themselves. Or perhaps they just never learned to consider anyone's feelings but their own.

It takes great strength of character to keep from hurting the other person back—no greater strength, however, than God promises those who trust in Him.

Jesus said, "Blessed are you when people insult you and persecute you, and falsely say all kinds of evil against you because of Me. Rejoice and be glad, for your reward in heaven is great."

With such encouragement, we can look for opportunities to pry the conversation door back open.

13 Be Agreeable

In his biography, Ben Franklin tells that he devised a list of virtues to live by.

"My list of virtues contained at first but twelve. But a Quaker friend, having kindly informed me that I was generally thought proud, that my pride showed itself frequently in conversation, that I was not content with being in the right when discussing any point, but was overbearing and rather insolent...I added humility to my list."

Win Every Argument

When you disagree with someone and are tempted to state your views in a way that may start an argument, then think of it this way—the argument is not with the other person. The argument is with yourself.

The disagreeable self wants to run a sword through the other person's opinion. The humble and wise self realizes that the argument is with the disagreeable self.

Turn the sword on the disagreeable self. Count it a victory when you overcome temptation to disagree with someone with harsh words or in a way that causes them unneeded pain or embarrassment.

That doesn't mean you have to agree with everything. It is just that knowing better than another person gives you power over that person. Be careful to exercise that power wisely.

Proverbs 17:14

The beginning of strife is like letting out water, So abandon the quarrel before it breaks out.

When We Disagree

When we disagree, we do not need to be disagreeable.
–Unknown

© 2003, 2004 Sweet Home Press

Conversation with Character

Besides, the other person may be right. How embarrassing to make a big deal about how you know better than another person, only to find later that you were wrong.

When people think of you as disagreeable, they may avoid having a conversation with you. You may miss a learning opportunity. They think, "Why bother telling him my opinion? He will just argue or be a know-it-all."

When faced with the temptation to be disagreeable, Ben Franklin learned to respond in a better way. [Parent: You may want to paraphrase Franklin in simpler words for younger children.]:

> "I made it a rule to forbear all direct contradiction to the sentiments of others, and all positive assertion of my own. I even forbade myself the use of every word or expression in the language that imported a fix'd opinion, such as 'certainly,' undoubtedly,' etc., and I adopted, instead of them, 'I conceive,' 'I apprehend,' or 'I imagine,' a thing to be so or so; or 'it appears to me at present.'"

When you disagree with someone, how do you say it? Has anyone ever become angry when you disagreed?

We disagree...in love.

Suggested Activity

One person should state an opinion that is probably incorrect (like "The weather is pleasant.") Another person should disagree, using words that are not disagreeable, as did Ben Franklin. Take turns until everyone seems to catch on.

(Note: You don't need to use Franklin's exact words. Give your opinion humbly in words that are natural for you.)

Franklin's Thirteen Virtues

1. Temperance
2. Silence
3. Order
4. Resolution
5. Frugality
6. Industry
7. Sincerity
8. Justice
9. Moderation
10. Cleanliness
11. Tranquility
12. Chastity
13. Humility

© 2003, 2004 Sweet Home Press

14 Be Loyal

What could be more loyal than a dog? Dogs removed from home have been known to walk hundreds of miles to get back to where they feel they belong. A dog well trained and cared for will do nearly anything for its owner. And never in recorded history has a dog ever told anyone about its owner's shortcomings.

This lesson encourages loyalty in conversation.

Be Loyal to Friends and Family

Never betray a confidence or tell anything that could embarrass another.

Think of one thing that your family knows about you that you would not want repeated to others. There are probably many things you don't want repeated outside your own family or circle of close friends.

Now think of how you would feel if everyone knew about that one thing. That is exactly how your brother or sister or parent or friend might feel if you told something personal and private about them.

Do not contradict a parent or older sibling about some factual detail around other people. For example, your sister might be telling a visitor about the six giraffes she saw at the zoo. There is no reason for you to interrupt her just to point out that it was only five giraffes.

If it is something important, ask your parent or sibling later about a possible error—

Proverbs 11:29

He who brings trouble on his family will inherit only wind, and the fool will be servant to the wise.

Better Left Unsaid

One of the very best rules of conversation is to never say anything which any of the company wish had been left unsaid.

- Jonathan Swift

© 2003, 2004 Sweet Home Press

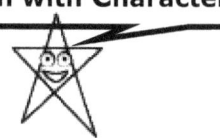

Conversation with Character

maybe you are wrong. In any case, don't embarrass a family member or friend. Don't make them look bad in front of others. Instead, protect them and show them respect in conversation with others.

Consider, too, what topics you select or steer the conversation toward. Some topics are sure to lead to embarrassment or awkwardness for another person. Think before you talk.

Suggested Activity

[Parent: Read a book that illustrates loyalty or discuss that character quality as illustrated in a book you have already read. A few of the many possibilities follow:]

- Beauty and the Beast
- Mike Mulligan and His Steam Shovel
- The Whipping Boy
- Frog and Toad are Friends
- Mrs. Frisby and the Rats of NIMH
- The Giving Tree
- The Velveteen Rabbit
- The Puppy Who Wanted a Boy
- The Biggest Bear
- The Lion, the Witch and The Wardrobe

Our daughters say some people ask them questions that threaten to "sabotage" loyalty to family. How does a child answer such questions?

See *Supplemental Materials S-14* for a list of awkward questions and possible answers.

A Matter of Attitude

[Parent: Read and discuss this section if conversation in your house is hindered by bad attitudes.]

Once we accept that disloyalty is wrong and see how it influences our conversation, it should not take long to develop habits of loyalty—unless, of course, there is another problem that first needs correction. That problem would be *attitude*.

If you have a bad attitude about family or friends, or even if you have a bad attitude about this lesson or the person teaching the lesson, you may find yourself being disloyal even when you know not to.

The best advice is to change your attitude. The next best advice is commit to be loyal even when you don't feel like it. Either way, you will be better off and those around you will appreciate your effort.

If you struggle with a bad attitude, humbly confess it to your parent(s). Ask God for help.

© 2003, 2004 Sweet Home Press

15 "Thank You" Pleases

Any car mechanic will tell you the most important thing to remember in caring for a car is to change the oil every 3,000 to 5,000 miles. A car engine runs better, smoother and lasts much longer when it always has fresh oil.

There is a kind of oil that humans need, too. It is the "please" and "thank you" oil. This lesson teaches the "please" and "thank you" habit.

Say "Please" and "Thank You"

One sure way to improve your relationship with others is by remembering to say "please" when you want something and "thank you" when you receive something.

This is probably not the first time you have been told to say "please" and "thank you," but has it become your habit? "Please" and "thank you" are the oil that makes friendship run better, smoother and longer.

When someone gives you a command: "Give me those potatoes", or an implied request: "I want some of those colored pencils," you probably don't feel inclined to give those potatoes or pencils. But when the same person ASKS, "Would you please pass the potatoes?" or "Please pass the colored pencils," you feel more like helping out.

Asking, rather than telling or commanding, and adding the word "please," make a big difference in how a person feels about helping others.

How pleasant it is, then, to hear "thank you" after doing someone a favor. Saying

---

Genesis 50:17

...And now, please forgive the transgression of the servants of the God of your father." And Joseph wept when they spoke to him.

Thank For Little

Who does not thank for little will not thank for much.

- Estonian Proverb

© 2003, 2004 Sweet Home Press

"thank you" (or "thanks") must be important, because the Bible tells us over and over to give thanks.

Suggested Activity

See Supplemental Materials S-15.

Play a variation of the traditional game "Mother May I," called "Mother May I, Please and Thank You." The variation for this exercise is explained in the right column.

As an additional or alternate activity, assign older children the task of finding examples of "please" and "thank you" in the Bible. Children can then read the verses out loud.

Here are some possible assignments:

- Find ten examples of someone saying "please" in the book of Genesis. [Parent: There are about 47 examples, depending on your translation.] Write the chapter and verse for each. Pick examples to read and explain to the rest of the family—telling who said it, who they said it to and why.

- Find ten times in the book of Psalms that speak of giving thanks. [Parent: There are about 60 examples, depending on your translation.] Write the chapter and verse for each. Pick examples to read and explain to the rest of the family.

[Parent: If ten examples seem too many for a child to find, give them some clues:

"Please" is found seven times in Genesis 24. Chapter 27 has four examples.

"Thanks" is found six times in Psalm 107. Chapter 118 has six examples.]

Note: Word counts are based on the New American Standard Bible®.

Conversation with Character

Mother May I, Please and Thank You

To play, modify the traditional "Mother May I," as follows:

The leader asks, "Billy, would you like to take three giant steps?" Billy then must say, "Mother (or Father if a boy is the leader), may I please?" If Billy does not say this, his turn is over. If he does, the leader can say, "Yes, you may," in which case Billy then takes three giant steps toward the finish line.

The leader can arbitrarily change his or her mind and say instead, "No, but would you like to take five baby steps?" Again, Billy must ask, "May I please?" If the leader says, "Yes, you may," then Billy may take five baby steps.

Billy must then say "Thank-you." If he forgets to say "thank-you," then Billy goes back.

The first child to reach the finish line wins.

© 2003, 2004 Sweet Home Press

16 Give and Receive Compliments

"Johnny!" the lady exclaimed, "You did such a wonderful job."

Johnny put his elbow over his eyes.

"I can't think of when I've seen someone work so hard," she went on.

Johnny crossed his legs and stared at the ground like someone who wants to disappear.

"Why," the kind lady wondered, "why has Johnny never learned how to graciously accept a compliment? After all, he's nearly 60 years old."

This lesson teaches how to gracefully give and receive compliments...while you are still young.

Give and Receive Compliments with Grace

Have you ever felt like Johnny? Do you rather dread hearing someone say nice things about you?

Do you ever want to say something nice to someone, but end up embarrassing yourself or saying things that aren't really true?

Well, you needn't have these problems if you will learn to graciously give and receive compliments.

First, you must learn to *receive* compliments. It isn't so hard. Look the person in the eye and simply say, "Thank you." That is all. If you argue that you are undeserv-

---

Song of Solomon 1:15

How beautiful you are,
my darling,
How beautiful you are!
Your eyes are like
doves.

Speak Well, Do Well

If you would be well spoken of, learn to be well-spoken; and having learnt to be well-spoken, strive also to be well-doing; so shall you succeed in being well spoken of.

- Epictetus

© 2003, 2004 Sweet Home Press

Conversation with Character

ing, that is like refusing to accept a gift. Or, if you go on at length about the compliment, it keeps the attention on yourself and makes you sound boastful or like you are fishing for more praise. If you must say more, then give God credit: "Thank God for making me able," or "God is good to me."

Now that you understand how to receive a compliment, consider how you can compliment others. Say what is true. [Parent: See the right column for a discussion of flattery.] Avoid offering compliments in ways that point out a person's shortcomings: "That is a great picture you just drew—not like most of the ones you've done."

The ability to graciously give and receive compliments is a mark of maturity.

Suggested Activity

Think of three sincere compliments you can give to someone else in the family (preferably to a brother or sister). Take turns complimenting each other. After each compliment, the person who received the compliment should look the other person in the eyes and say "Thank you."

[Parent: Don't let children by with silliness or flattery.]

[Parent: Provide a container for each child (box, can, etc.) and label it with their name. Optionally, have each child decorate a "permanent" container and make this a long term activity.] During the day, each person should write at least one compliment to each other family member and put it in their container. Read these aloud together in the evening.

> Dad, you're a supernova!
> Mom, you could run rings around Saturn!

The Problem with Flattery

Flattery is saying you admire something about a person when you don't really mean it or when, at best, you are exaggerating.

If we genuinely like someone, but can't think of a genuine compliment at the moment, we sometimes resort to flattery. But flattery is a lie and should be avoided. Psalm 12:3 says, "May the LORD cut off all flattering lips…"

To respond in the best way to someone else's flattery, it helps to understand the flatterer's motives. If the purpose of flattery is selfish—to win a favor from you—then it is okay not to accept the words the way you would a true compliment. You have reason to be cautious about what comes next from that person. You might say, "Thank you," and try to end the conversation or go on to a better topic. Or you might say, "Thank you, but that is not really true."

© 2003, 2004 Sweet Home Press

17 Take A Good Call
(On the telephone)

We once lived in Austria, where people speak German. Because our German was not very good, we dreaded hearing the phone ring. We misunderstood most of what we heard and found ourselves so tongue-tied by the experience that we could barely answer.

Many children feel that way the first couple of times they answer the telephone. This lesson offers a little instruction and practice to take away the dread—unless, that is, the call happens to come from *Austria!*

Take a Good Telephone Call

When you answer the telephone, give a cheery "hello" or answer the phone in the way your parents advise. If the call is for someone else, tell the caller, "Just a minute, please. I'll go get him/her." Then put the receiver down gently. Clanging it on a countertop or dropping it on the floor is most unpleasant to the ears on the other end of the line.

Don't Yell—go tell. If you yell across the house to tell your mother she is wanted on the telephone, it blasts out the eardrum of the caller, and it is rude to both the caller and your mother. Don't do it! Instead, move closer to the person whose attention you are trying to attract.

If the person you ask for is not there or not able to come to the phone, say "(Mom) can't come to the phone right now. Would you like to leave a message?" It's handy to

---

2 Timothy 4:2

...be ready in season and out of season...

Expecting the Unexpected

In Britain it (the telephone) will connect you to all sorts of people you had no intention of speaking to in the first place.

- Robert B. Semple Jr.

© 2003, 2004 Sweet Home Press

keep a pencil and paper near the phone. Be sure to write down the caller's name and number. If you take a message, make sure you remember to deliver it!

Never give out personal information. Don't tell strangers that your parents are not home. Never give out your address or other information about your family.

Neither does the caller need to know that your mother or father are in the bathroom! A simple "He/she is unable to come to the phone right now" will be a good answer.

When you hang up, put the phone down gently. Banging the phone down tells the other person you are angry. Angry is not a good way to end a conversation, and banging the phone down shows a lack of self-control.

Suggested Activity

Practice receiving telephone calls. A child can receive a call on a house phone from a parent who calls from a car phone, or you can use "pretend" phones.

Discuss how to improve the conversation and try it again. Use different scenarios, like:

- A friend or relative who wants to chat
- The same person calls asking to speak to someone who is not available
- A stranger asks questions
- The repairman leaves a message
- A salesperson gets pushy
- Someone calls a wrong number

Now, that's a wrong number.

555-OOPS

© 2003, 2004 Sweet Home Press

Conversation with Character

Taking Is Harder Than Making

Many people find it more difficult to receive a call than to make one. When you make a call, you know why you are calling and what you will probably say.

When you answer the telephone, you have no idea who is calling, unless you have "caller ID" service. Even then, you can only guess at the reason for the call.

You generally make calls when you feel prepared. Whereas, your phone often rings when least expected and most inconvenient.

Parents...

You may want to discuss any special telephone calls you might receive at your house, like calls for a home business, calls that may require taking certain actions and calls from that "problem person."

Most experts say it is best to "just hang up" on crank callers.

18 Make A Good Call
(On the telephone)

Making the first successful telephone call is a big hurdle for most children, and it isn't always easy for older children and adults. This lesson helps all on their way.

Make a Good Telephone Call

Before you pick up a telephone to make a call, think through what you will do and say and how to handle the unexpected. Make sure you have the number in front of you. Make sure no one is on the phone in another room. Think through what you want to say and especially what words you will use to begin the conversation.

When the person you are calling does not answer the phone quickly, be patient. Give them time to get to the phone.

When someone answers, introduce yourself right away, even if you think they will recognize your voice. Even a family member may not recognize your voice on the phone instantly.

Say "Hello. This is (full name)." The family you call may know more than one person with your first name, so use your family name, also.

If the person who answers is not the one you want, ask if you may speak to that person. "May I speak to Jeff, please?" is better than "Is Jeff home?" If he is not available, you may leave a message and/or you might ask when it would be a convenient time to call back.

Pick your times well. Avoid very early and

Colossians 4:5

Conduct yourselves with wisdom toward outsiders, making the most of the opportunity.

People Were Cleaner Then?

The bathtub was invented in 1850 and the telephone in 1875. In other words, if you had been living in 1850, you could have sat in the bathtub for 25 years without having to answer the phone.

-Bill DeWitt

© 2003, 2004 Sweet Home Press

very late. Family habits vary, so it is best to ask your friends what time is best to call. If you don't know, some general guidelines might be: Don't call before 8:00 AM or after 9:00 PM, or at typical meal times.

Dial very carefully to avoid wrong numbers. If you DO reach the wrong number, don't be one of those rude people who just hang up! You may want to verify the number with the person you called, so you know whether the number itself is incorrect or if you just misdialed. Ask "Is this 999-1234?" Apologize! Saying "I must have the wrong number. I'm so sorry to have disturbed you" only takes a few seconds and is considerate of the person you have troubled.

Keep conversations with busy people (like homeschooling moms) as brief as possible.

Give the other person your full attention. Watching TV, pecking on a computer keyboard, eating, or carrying on two conversations at the same time tells that person, "You are not worth my full attention."

And be sure to say "Good-bye" before you hang up!

Suggested Activity

Practice receiving telephone calls in the same manner described in chapter 17, **Take a Good Call**. Use different scenarios, like calling

- To invite a friend over
- The store to ask how to get there
- To leave a message for someone
- To ask a favor
- To chat with a friend or family member

Be creative with the activity and have some fun.

Conversation with Character

More Telephone Tips

Keep the receiver about 1/2 to 1 inch away from your lips. Don't place your mouth on the receiver.

Make an extra effort to speak distinctly. The listener has no facial expressions or body movements to aid in understanding.

Smile when you talk; it shows up in your voice!

Parents...

Discuss

- When it might be appropriate to call 911 (emergency), as well as how serious it is to misuse emergency numbers.
- How to dial a long distance number and the costs involved.
- Etiquette for using someone else's phone.
- The problem with listening in on a conversation.

© 2003, 2004 Sweet Home Press

19 Pour Water on Gossip

Have you ever heard a siren and seen that big fire truck streak down the street toward a puff of smoke in the sky? Have you seen a firefighter up close and marveled at the impressive uniform and equipment? Have you heard stories of how a firefighter's bravery saved others or how he gave his life trying to help others?

Each of us is called to be a firefighter, pouring water on a dangerous wildfire called "gossip." This lesson teaches gossip prevention, detection and extinction.

Fight the Gossip Wildfire

Gossip is anything told about a person that makes them seem foolish or that raises doubts about their character. Gossip has no place in the language of God's kingdom and does nothing but harm in this world.

In the lesson *Be Loyal*, we talked about not contradicting or causing embarrassment to a friend or family member. Gossip is certainly disloyal, but gossip might be about anyone, not just family or friends. Some people gossip about those they have never met.

Gossiping is disloyal, but more than that, it often has little regard for the truth. Gossip also spreads like a wildfire. Once gossip spreads, there seems no stopping it and no undoing it. No wonder the Bible three times calls

---

Proverbs 11:13

He who goes about as a talebearer reveals secrets,
But he who is trustworthy conceals a matter.

The Brilliant Conversationalist

A gossip is one who talks to you about others; a bore is one who talks to you about himself; and a brilliant conversationalist is one who talks to you about yourself.

- Lisa Kirk

those who gossip "malicious." (I Timothy 3:11; II Timothy 3:3; Titus 2:3).

How should we respond when we hear gossip? The first rule is "Don't entertain gossip." This means don't listen to it and encourage it. Change the subject if possible. If you know for sure that some of the gossip is false, say so without getting into an argument or encouraging the gossiper to tell even more.

The second rule is "Don't repeat gossip to others." When it comes to gossip, be the firefighter who pours water on the flames before they can spread. It is a tough job, requiring bravery, but this is what God expects of us.

Suggested Activity

To illustrate how even well-meaning talebearers get it wrong, play telephone.

Ask a child to whisper the following story to another child. Have that child whisper the story to a third child. Have the third child whisper it to a fourth child (or to as many children with which your family is blessed). Have the last child repeat the story out loud for everyone to hear.

> *Helen said she would make popcorn for the whole family, but her brothers said they didn't want any. Don ate apples and Greg ate soup. Alan ate nothing at all. But when the popcorn was made 25 minutes later, everyone smelled it and wanted some.*

Now read the original story and discuss how it changed as it went from person to person. [Parent: If it fits in the day, you might make popcorn, just to make it fun. You might also shorten the story for younger children.]

Where Gossip is Welcome

Small towns are famous for gossip—probably because so many people know the same people and families. Most everyone is interested in hearing the latest news about the people they know.

Among the places known for gossip are the beauty salon, barbershop, post office, local cafe and drug store.

Where do you hear gossip? Discuss how to avoid being a party to gossip.

When does a star rain? When it is putting out gossip.

© 2003, 2004 Sweet Home Press

20 End the Conversation

When my parents said it was "time to go," signaling the end of a visit to my Aunt and Uncle, I knew we were in for another 20 minutes of grown-up conversation between the couch and the door—just enough time for my cousins and me to play another round of whatever we were playing.

End It Gracefully

Some people are good at ending conversations in a graceful way—not too abruptly and not too drawn out. For many, however, bringing a conversation to a close, especially a long conversation, is a difficult chore.

There is the person who just can't stop talking. When it seems the conversation will end, it is their cue to bring up all of the topics they wanted to discuss. Or there are the two tenacious people, neither of whom can part without having the final say.

Less tedious, though just as unsatisfactory, is the person or persons who don't know how to gracefully end a conversation, so they just end it with a grunt or a sudden good-bye.

If your visit has been very long or the conversation has delved deeply into personal feelings or controversy, allow time at the end to speak of lighter matters. Try to leave with emotions calmed and, as far as possible, at peace with all.

Acts 21:5

When our days there were ended, we left and started on our journey, while they all, with wives and children, escorted us until we were out of the city. After kneeling down on the beach and praying, we said farewell to one another.

Such Sweet Sorrow

Parting is such sweet sorrow
That I shall say good night till it be morrow.

-William Shakespeare

© 2003, 2004 Sweet Home Press

If the conversation has been so good that it seems to you no one wants to part, be willing to let those final words of farewell be the last words, anyway. It is responsible use of time to let a conversation end at the proper moment.

If it is merely time for you to leave the room or table, wait for a comfortable break in the conversation. Stand and say "Excuse me please. It was very nice talking with you," or something to that effect. Avoid abruptness, which might make the person feel they have offended you in some way.

Ending a conversation requires social skills that must be observed, learned and practiced. So begin observing how adults bring conversations to a close, and learn from the best examples. Make a conscious effort to practice ending conversations in a way that wastes no one's time and yet leaves each person feeling satisfied at having been together.

First impressions are lasting, but final impressions can last a lifetime.

Suggested Activity

Recall times when you thought a conversation ended well and times when it seemed to end unsatisfactorily. Discuss what you recall that made the difference. Think of people you know who do it well and discuss why.

Spend the week observing how conversations end. Discuss later with each other what you have observed and what you tried that seemed to work.

Some Final Rules

Jesus summed up many rules by saying simply "**Do unto others** what you would have them do unto you."

Much of the art of courteous conversation can be summed up by the following:

Think before you speak. If you take time to put your thoughts together rather than blurting something out, many errors will be avoided.

Have a teachable spirit. Enter into a conversation desiring to learn from the other person rather than to impress them with your own knowledge.

Some little characters say good-bye at sunrise.

21 Give Respect and Honor

[Parent: If any lesson deserves extra attention, it is this one. Give this special four-page lesson as much time and effort as needed.]

Honor Your Elders

Children are not equal to adults; not socially, not physically, not in experience, and not in responsibility. Because of these differences, children should not talk to adults the same way they talk to other children.

The Bible actually says that *everyone* owes honor and respect to someone. Romans 13:7 says, "Give everyone what you owe him: If you owe taxes, pay taxes; if revenue, then revenue; if respect, then respect; if honor, then honor." Children must honor and be respectful to everyone in authority over them: to parents, teachers, government officials, police officers, babysitters and others.

Most importantly, God commands that children show respect to their parents. The fifth commandment says, "'Honor your father and your mother, as the LORD your God has commanded you, that your days may be prolonged and that it may go well with you on the land which the LORD your God gives you."

Young people are to show respect also to older adults. Hear God's heart on the matter

---

Ephesians 6:2-3

Honor your father and mother (which is the first commandment with a promise), so that it may be well with you, and that you may live long on the earth.

Talk with the Wise

A single conversation with a wise man is better than ten years of study.

-Chinese Proverb

© 2003, 2004 Sweet Home Press

in Leviticus 19:32: "Rise in the presence of the aged, show respect for the elderly and revere your God. I am the LORD." After all, people who have lived a long time are much wiser than the young, so we can learn much by respecting what they say. This is clear in Job 12:12: "Is not wisdom found among the aged? Does not long life bring understanding?"

Don't Be Overly Familiar

Many of the world's languages have special words that younger people use when speaking to adults, or that anyone uses when speaking to a stranger or to someone in authority. For example, if a German child says, "How are you?" to another child, he will say, "Wie gehts du?" (pronounced like "vee gates doo") But if the child speaks to an adult, they will say, "Wie geht es Ihnen?" (pronounced like "vee gate es eenen"). Spanish students can probably tell how that language does the same thing. It would be scandalous for a child to use the wrong words in addressing an adult.

Using Special Titles

While English does not have that same clear distinction, there are tools in our language with the same effect. Soldiers address superior officers as "Sir." A patient will normally address their physician as "Doctor," for example, "Doctor Anderson." Yet, soldiers speak to equals in a more familiar way, using first and/or last name, as might doctors addressing doctors of equal standing.

School students generally call teachers by titles, such as "Mrs. Green," or "Mr. Sanchez." Even adult students address their teachers this way, out of respect.

Conversation with Character

Showing Respect Around the World

In Asia, instead of a handshake, a person will bow. The person with lower status bows more deeply.

In Greece, the highest term of respect, usually reserved for monastery abbots, is *geronda*, which means "old man."

In South Africa, when speaking to another person, hands are kept out of the pockets. To do otherwise is thought rude and disrespectful.

In Europe, men traditionally walk to the left side of the ladies. They generally enter a restaurant ahead of the lady, to lead the way to the table.

In Finland, a man greeting someone on the street should raise his hat. In the cold of winter, a touch to the brim is sufficient.

© 2003, 2004 Sweet Home Press

21 Give Respect and Honor

In our home, adults are addressed as Mr., Miss or Mrs., Aunt or Uncle, Sir, Ma'am and the like. This is clearly different from the way our children address their peers.

In a Manner of Speaking

Beyond titles or special words, the manner in which a child speaks to peers may not be appropriate when speaking to adults. A playful "Billy, you big dummy," may or may not be acceptable with a playmate, depending on family rules. However, "Dad, you big dummy" is never acceptable, no matter how jokingly it is said.

Sarcastic banter, like "Ha-ha, that was so funny, I forgot to laugh," might be appropriate with a sibling or friend, but not with an adult. This manner of speaking shows inappropriate familiarity.

Children should not yell at an adult to come to them. They show respect by going to the adult, recognizing their greater position.

Children must never correct an adult without first obtaining permission to do so. For instance, "May I ask you about _____?"

It is unseemly for a child to criticize an adult, even when their behavior is clearly wrong. Such adult examples may include a politician who takes ungodly stands on issues or a rude sales clerk. A child might evaluate the behavior and speak of it to parents in private, but a child should not deride an adult for their behavior.

Tone of voice is especially important when speaking to an adult. Sarcasm, whining, or a loud or angry voice are all disrespectful. Physical actions such as rolling eyes, stomping feet, sighs, door slamming, intentional yawns and the like all show disrespect.

Show Humility

A teachable spirit is important in everyone, and all the more in a child. No one enjoys a "know it all." Worse, yet, is a child who presumes to know more than an adult.

A child should never talk about anything they don't know, except to ask questions so they can learn! Children must show respect for their elders. Elders have much more life experience and were educated before the child was even born!

Suggested Activities

Read the following statements and play the "Beep" game. Say "beep" whenever a statement *is not* appropriate for a child to say to an adult. Applaud when the statement *is* appropriate.

[Parent: Here are some statements to get you started. Add some of your own. Once children understand the game well, you might let them think of some statements to try

© 2003, 2004 Sweet Home Press

Conversation with Character

with each other. Don't forget to have fun.]

- May I please touch this glass hummingbird? (applause)
- Give me that book! (beep)
- May I go now? (applause)
- But I don't want to! (beep)
- Boy, our neighbor sure is rude. You know what he did? (beep)
- Keep your shirt on. I'll be there after I get a drink. (beep)
- Hey, Fred, how ya doin'? (beep)
- Good morning, Mrs. Smith. How are you? (applause)
- (When an adult asks for something)
  Say please! (said jokingly) (beep)
- Come here! (beep)
- I'm going out to play now (as opposed to asking permission). (beep)
- My mom did the dumbest thing yesterday. She... (beep)
- (at the dinner table) I don't like green beans. (beep)
- Yes, Dad (or Father). (applause)
- (after an adult greets you) <Silence> (beep)
- Is there anything else you need me to do or may I go play now? (applause)
- May I offer my vote on where we go to dinner? (applause)
- Look at me! (beep)

A practical way to practice respect is by remembering to "*stop, look* and *listen*" whenever an adult speaks.

Stop—Don't just keep walking or talking.

Look—Lift your head and look them in the eyes so they know you are paying attention.

Listen—Think about what the grownup is saying.

Now find in *Supplemental Materials S-21* a traffic light. This light reminds us to stop, look and listen when an adult speaks. Color the light and then hang it up as a reminder through the week.

[Parent: Children, like all of us, benefit from practice. Give your child conversation assignments. You might require, for example, that the next time you are with the church, your child greet one adult and engage in conversation for at least one minute. Later, praise your child for trying and talk about what happened. What worked well and what can be learned from the experience?]

22 Prepare for Group-Speak
(an optional parent-planned lesson)

[Parent: Unlike the others, this lesson is meant to guide you in preparing your children for conversation in group settings. Rather than read the lesson to your children, take time to plan how you can guide them in the specific group situations they face.]

Groups are where we gain our public identity and a sense of belonging. Every parent wants their children to be welcome and thought well of in such places, be they extended family gatherings, weddings, church meetings, sports, music groups, etc.

One thing home educated children often lack is experience in group settings. They may be accustomed to sitting on the floor barefoot during "school time," speaking up without permission. Enroll them in a special classroom-style course (science, art, music, etc.) and a parent may be embarrassed at how unprepared their children are for a group setting.

In What Group Settings Do Your Children Speak?

First, to clarify, this is not a lesson on public speaking. This is a lesson on navigating the often complex social interchange that takes place in a group.

Make a list of the group settings your children find themselves in where they have opportunity to enter into discussion, answer questions or make com-

---

Deuteronomy 32:1

Give ear, O heavens, and let me speak;
And let the earth hear the words of my mouth.

I Don't Know Half of You

I don't know half of you half as well as I should like; and I like less than half of you half as well as you deserve.

-Bilbo Baggins
in Lord of the Rings
by J. R. R. Tolkien

© 2003, 2004 Sweet Home Press

ments. If there are many, pick a few of the most important, or focus on one at a time, starting with the most important gathering.

Alternately, there may be an upcoming special gathering for which you must prepare children.

Things to Consider

Consider the official or unspoken rules of a group gathering. Perhaps Aunt Stella is always in charge and if you do it her way, you are probably okay. Maybe a group with a specific purpose, like a band or 4-H club, has a set way of doing things, with certain times to speak and to remain silent.

You know your children. How can you prepare them to communicate in the group setting so they become known for their best qualities?

Plan Your Lesson(s)

If planning for a new or special sort of gathering, like a wedding, reunion or special church function, tell children who will be there, what is likely to happen, how to handle introductions and what the basic family guidelines are for participation. For example, do they need to ask a parent's permission before saying something in the group setting? You might need to review how to handle the more familiar settings where improvement is in order.

You know your children and you know your gatherings. Plan this as a regular lesson in the curriculum and/or make this a recurring topic as children grow and groups change.

Conversation with Character

Keep It Brief and Relevant

It bears reminding children that group settings provide limited time for speaking one's mind.

If a question is asked, encourage children to answer as clearly and briefly as possible, leaving out unnecessary details, which may be of interest to them, but not likely of interest to the group.

Also, remind children to select words carefully and speak them clearly, as there is a good chance someone in a group will misunderstand.

The time a group spends listening to one person is very valuable. Help your children be valued members of that group.

Don't overlook the obvious. Home educated children may not know to raise their hand in a group.

© 2003, 2004 Sweet Home Press

Supplemental Materials

Supplemental materials augment various lessons in this book. To find your way around, note how each section corresponds to a lesson, e.g. section S-05 corresponds to lesson 5.

© 2003, 2004 Sweet Home Press

Supplemental Materials
S-01a

Conversation with Character

This material goes with Lesson 01

Art	Family	Tradition	Free Time	Friends
Season	Music	*(instructions)*	Pet	Hobby
Person	Country		Book	Learn
Bible	Project	This Week	Trip	History

Cut out the cards and put them in a pile, face down. Take turns drawing a card and thinking of a conversation starter question using the word on the card. Any form of the word is allowed. Example: "Do you live in the country?", "What country would you like to visit?" etc. If time allows, let each person take turns asking questions. [Parent: If time allows, let each person answer the questions they are asked.]

© 2003, 2004 Sweet Home Press

Supplemental Materials
S-01b

This material goes with Lesson 01
(However, you may want to use this material
at other times, with friends and family.)

Conversation with Character

Asking questions is a good way to get to know a person. Next time you visit someone, use this list to take turns answering each question. Listen patiently to what each person has to say. Don't criticize. That way, everyone feels cared for.

Getting To Know Each Other

- What is something you have always wanted to do that you will probably never get to do?

- What are your hobbies?

- What is your favorite season and why?

- What does your name mean?

- What type of artwork do you enjoy?

- If you could spend a year anywhere, where would you spend it?

- What is some of your favorite music?

- Would you enjoy: living the same place your whole life, constantly traveling or living a few different places?

- Would you rather visit: the beach, mountains or historical sites? Why?

- What person in history would you like to spend a day with?

- If you could own any animal, which would you choose?

- What do you like to do when you are traveling in the car?

© 2003, 2004 Sweet Home Press

Supplemental Materials
S-03a

This material goes with Lesson 03

Conversation with Character

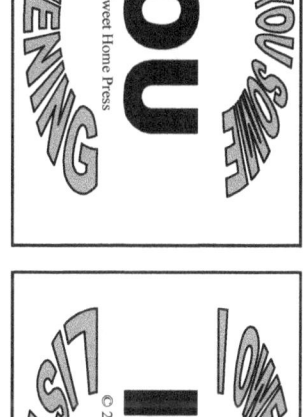

© 2003, 2004 Sweet Home Press

Supplemental Materials
S-03a

This material goes with Lesson 03

Conversation with Character

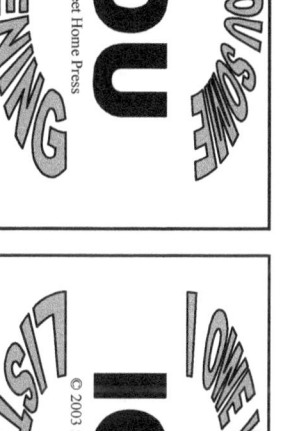

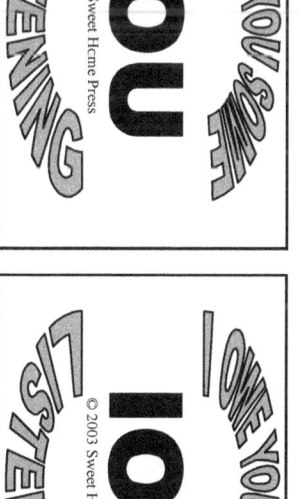

© 2003, 2004 Sweet Home Press

S-03a Supplemental Materials — This material goes with Lesson 03 — Conversation with Character

© 2003, 2004 Sweet Home Press

Out-Ouch

by Bethany Notgrass
Used with permission.

Listen in on this conversation:

> Bonnie: Oh Jenny! Did you break your leg?
> Jenny: Yes, last week when my family went skiing.
> Bonnie: Ow. I broke my leg falling out of a tree five years ago. I broke my arm, too. Both were compound fractures.
> Jenny: Whoa, that must have been painful.
> Bonnie: Yeah, the breaks were so bad I had to stay in casts for ten weeks.
> Jenny: Really? I think I'll get this off in about five more weeks.
> Bonnie: That shouldn't be too bad. I guess skiing isn't as dangerous as climbing trees, huh?
> Jenny: No, I guess not.

Bonnie did what my dad calls "out-ouching"

> Jenny: She was sorry about Jenny's accident, but just happened to mention that an accident she had experienced was much worse.
> Bonnie communicated: "I know just how you feel, only more so."

Do you think Jenny was comforted when she left this conversation? Sympathy is something we are to have for others. It is to be pure, unselfish sympathy that reveals itself in kind words and actions. Being human, it comes naturally to begin thinking of ourselves after managing sympathy for, maybe, three seconds. Another person is having trouble? We may easily think "Oh...that's too bad. I sure know how it feels. Last year, I...." That "I" can creep in before we realize it.

Sometimes it is helpful to tell people that you understand what they are going through. Notice the difference in this conversation:

> Amy: I'm really sorry about your Grandmother's passing, Dana.
> Dana: Thank you, Amy.
> Amy: I know she was very important to you, wasn't she?
> Dana: Yes, I miss her a lot. I'm still having a hard time.
> Amy: When my grand-

mother died, it was a long time before I stopped crying every day. It's okay to still be upset. You loved her and you'll always miss her.

Dana: It's nice to know you understand how I'm feeling.

Amy: What was one of your favorite things about her?

Dana: When I would visit her, she would take me around the yard...

Amy had experienced losing an important person in her life, and it helped Dana to know Amy understood. Still, Amy kept the focus on Dana and her loss, rather than putting the focus on herself.

People need time to mourn and, as Christians, we can represent Christ by being a voice of comfort and validating their pain by simple sympathy. Let me remind you of a poignant Bible verse that carries far-reaching meaning in a simple sentence:

Rejoice with those who rejoice, weep with those who weep - Romans 12:15.

Let's stay away from out-ouching people who are suffering. Let's remember to put others first, and show them the comfort of Christ.

Bear one another's burdens, and thus fulfill the law of Christ. - Gal. 6:2

@ Bethany Notgrass

Bethany Notgrass graduated from her family's homeschool in 1999. She began the **amie** network in 2001 to encourage young women. Bethany works with The Notgrass Company (notgrass.com), the homeschool publishing business owned by her family, and helps manage the household. She enjoys baking, music, reading, and embroidery. Her dog is named Star, and her computer is named Herbert. Contact her at bethany@notgrass.com.

© 2003, 2004 Sweet Home Press

Conversation with Character

Supplemental Materials **S-05**

This material goes with Lesson 05

I do not need to say everything I think or feel.

Poster arranged by Amy J. Smith

© 2003, 2004 Sweet Home Press

Supplemental Materials
S-10

This material goes with Lesson 10

Conversation with Character

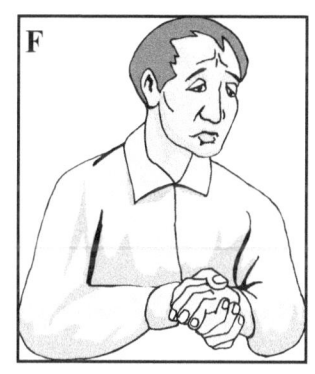

Match Expressions to Body Language

These people aren't speaking at all. Yet they are all definitely communicating something! What does their body language tell you?

Match each person with all communications you think they could be giving. There may be more than one answer.

1. I'm angry.
2. I wish you would stop talking!
3. I like you.
4. I'm ashamed.
5. I'm really thinking about what you are saying.
6. I don't trust you.
7. I'm sad.
8. I'm bored.
9. I'm thinking about something else and not listening to you at all.
10. I'm so sorry.
11. I'm hurt.
12. I'm so glad to see you.

Here are the answers. Can you think of any more?

A: 8   C: 2   E: 5   G: 4, 7, 11
B: 1, 6   D: 3, 12   F: 7, 10, 11   H: 9, 8

© 2003, 2004 Sweet Home Press

Supplemental Materials
S-11

Conversation with Character

This material goes with Lesson 11

Excerpts from the 110 "Rules of Civility and Decent Behaviour in Company and Conversation"
by George Washington

1. Every action done in company ought to be with some sign of respect to those that are present.

4. In the presence of others, sing not to yourself with a humming voice, or drum with your fingers or feet.

5. If you cough, sneeze, sigh, or yawn, do it not loud but privately, and speak not in your yawning, but put your handkerchief or hand before your face and turn aside.

6. Sleep not when others speak; sit not when others stand; speak not when you should hold your peace; walk not on when others stop.

7. Put not off your clothes in the presence of others, nor go out your chamber half dressed.

8. At play and attire, it's good manners to give place to the last comer, and affect not to speak louder than ordinary.

11. Shift not yourself in the sight of others, nor gnaw your nails.

> Because some of Washington's Rules don't pertain to conversation, some were lost through damage to the original manuscript, and since a few are not suitable for all children, we selected for this edition those most appropriate to this topic and audience.

12. Shake not the head, feet, or legs; roll not the eyes; lift not one eyebrow higher than the other, wry not the mouth, and bedew no man's face with your spittle by (approaching too near) him (when) you speak.

14. Turn not your back to others, especially in speaking; jog not the table or desk on which another reads or writes; lean not upon anyone.

16. Do not puff up the cheeks, loll not out the tongue with the hands, or beard, thrust out the lips, or bite them, or keep the lips too open or too close.

17. Be no flatterer, neither play with any that delight not to be played withal.

© 2003, 2004 Sweet Home Press

18. Read no letter, books, or papers in company, but when there is a necessity for the doing of it, you must ask leave; come not near the books or writings of another so as to read them unless desired, or give your opinion of them unasked,- also look not nigh when another is writing a letter.

19. Let your countenance be pleasant but in serious matters somewhat grave.

20. The gestures of the body must be suited to the discourse you are upon.

22. Show not yourself glad at the misfortune of another though he were your enemy.

25. Superfluous compliments and all affectation of ceremonies are to be avoided, yet where due they are not to be neglected.

33. They that are in dignity or in office have in all places precedency, but whilst they are young, they ought to respect those that are their equals in birth or other qualities, though they have no public charge.

34. It is good manners to prefer them to whom we speak before ourselves, especially if they be above us, with whom in no sort we ought to begin.

35. Let your discourse with men of business be short and comprehensive.

38. In visiting the sick, do not presently play the physician if you be not knowing therein.

39. In writing or speaking, give to every person his due title according to his degree and the custom of the place.

40. Strive not with your superior in argument, but always submit your argument to others with modesty.

41. Undertake not to teach your equal in the art himself professes.

43. Do not express joy before one sick in pain, for that contrary passion will aggravate his misery.

45. Being to advise or reprehend any one, consider whether it ought to be in public or in private, and presently or at some other time; in what terms to do it; and in reproving show no signs of cholor but do it with all sweetness and mildness.

46. Take all admonitions thankfully in what time or place soever given, but afterwards not being culpable take a time and place convenient to let him know it that gave them.

Conversation with Character

47. Mock not nor jest at any thing of importance. Break no jests that are sharp, biting,- and if you deliver any thing witty and pleasant, abstain from laughing thereat yourself.

48. Where in (wherein) you reprove another be unblameable yourself, -for example is more prevalent than precepts,

49. Use no reproachful language against any one; neither curse nor revile.

50. Be not hasty to believe flying reports to the disparagement of any.

54. Play not the peacock, looking every where about you, to see if you be well decked, if your shoes fit well, if your stockings sit neatly and clothes handsomely.

56. Associate yourself with men of good quality if you esteem your own reputation; for 'tis better to be alone than in bad company.

58. Let your conversation be without malice or envy, for 'tis a sign of a tractable and commendable nature, and in all causes of passion permit reason to govern.

59. Never express anything unbecoming, nor act against the rules before your inferiors.

61. Utter not base and frivolous things among grave and learned men, nor very difficult questions or subjects among the ignorant, or things hard to be believed; stuff not your discourse with sentences among your betters nor equals.

62. Speak not of doleful things in a time of mirth or at the table; speak not of melancholy things or death and wounds, and if others mention them, change if you can the discourse; tell not your dream, but to your intimate.

65. Speak not injurious words neither in jest nor earnest; scoff at none although they give occasion.

These maxims were so fully exemplified in George Washington's life that biographers have regarded them as formative influences in the development of his character.

During the days before mere hero worship had given place to understanding and comprehension of the fineness of Washington's character, of his powerful influence among men, and of the epoch-making nature of the issues he so largely shaped, it was assumed that Washington himself composed the maxims, or at least that he compiled them.

It is a satisfaction to find that his consideration for others, his respect for and deference to those deserving such treatment, his care of his own body and tongue, and even his reverence for his Maker, all were early inculcated in him by precepts which were the common practice in decent society the world over. These very maxims had been in use in France for a century and a half, and in England for a century, before they were set as a task for the schoolboy Washington.

(Excerpt from an introduction written by Charles Moore in 1926 for Boston and New York: Houghton Mifflin Company.)

© 2003, 2004 Sweet Home Press

66. Be not froward but friendly and courteous, the first to salute, hear, and answer; and be not pensive when it's a time to converse.

67. Detract not from others, neither be excessive in commanding.

69. If two contend together take not the part of either unconstrained, and be not obstinate in your own opinion; in things indifferent be of the major side.

70. Reprehend not the imperfections of others, for that belongs to parents, masters, and superiors.

71. Gaze not on the marks or blemishes of others and ask not how they came. What you may speak in secret to your friend, deliver not before others.

72. Speak not in an unknown tongue in company but in your own language and that as those of quality do and not as the vulgar; sublime matters treat seriously-

73. Think before you speak; pronounce not imperfectly, nor bring out your words too hastily, but orderly and distinctly.

74. When another speaks, be attentive yourself; and disturb not the audience. If any hesitate in his words, help him not nor prompt him without desired; interrupt him not, nor answer him till his speech has ended.

75. (damaged manuscript) If a person of quality comes in while you're conversing, it's handsome to repeat what was said before.

76. While you are talking, point not with your finger at him of whom you discourse, nor approach too near him to whom you talk especially to his face.

77. Treat with men at fit times about business and whisper not in the company of others.

78. Make no comparisons and if any of the company be commended for any brave act of virtue, commend not another for the same.

79. Be not apt to relate news if you know not the truth thereof. In discoursing of things you have heard, name not your author always; a secret discover not.

80. Be not tedious in discourse or in reading unless you find the company pleased therewith.

84. When your superiors talk to anybody neither speak nor laugh.

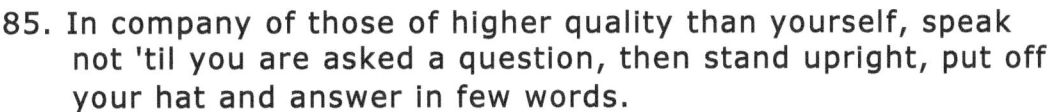 

85. In company of those of higher quality than yourself, speak not 'til you are asked a question, then stand upright, put off your hat and answer in few words.

86. In disputes, be not so desirous to overcome as not to give liberty to one to deliver his opinion and submit to the judgment of the major part, specially if they are judges of the dispute.

88. Be not diverse in discourse; make not many digressions; nor repeat often the same manner of discourse.

89. Speak not evil of the absent, for it is unjust.

98. Drink not nor talk with your mouth full; neither gaze about you while you are a drinking.

100. Cleanse not your teeth with the tablecloth, napkin, fork, or knife; but if others do it, let it be done without a peep to them.

105. Be not angry at table whatever happens and if you have reason to be so, show it not but on a cheerful countenance especially if there be strangers, for good humor makes one dish of meat and whey.

107. If others talk at table be attentive but talk not with meat in your mouth.

108. When you speak of God or his Attributes, let it be seriously; reverence, honor and obey your natural parents although they be poor.

110. Labor to keep alive in your breast that little spark of celestial fire called conscience.

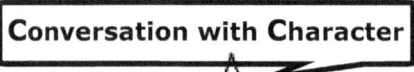

This material goes with Lesson 14

Sabotage!

by Bethany G. Smith and Amy J. Smith
of Sweet Home Press

People sometimes ask children awkward questions that threaten to *sabotage* their efforts to be loyal to family—questions like, "Is your sister mean?" These questions come from adults and from other children. Often, they are just trying to be funny. Adults are trying to relate to the child. You should try to answer such questions in a respectful way, but don't let them sabotage your family! Here are some questions that children have asked us, along with some loyal, but polite answers. If someone gets too nosy, or makes you feel uncomfortable, it is perfectly all right to not answer and to go to your parents for help.

Awkward Questions Other Children Ask	Tactful Answers You Might Give
1. Who do you like best of your friends?	1. I like all my friends. -or- My friends are all so special, I couldn't choose!
2. Your sister's bossy isn't she?	2. My sister loves me. -or- She's the best!
3. Boy, your parents are strict!	3. I'm glad they do what's best for me.
4. Why don't your parents let you watch that/ do that/read that?	4. Because they don't think it would be best for me right now.
5. (Usually comes up when playing a party game like punchboard.) What's one of the dumbest things your parents/siblings/friends,	5. I wouldn't like someone else to tell the dumbest thing I ever did—but I don't mind telling on myself! Do you know what I did
6. Who do you think is prettier, my mom/sister or yours? -or- Don't you think my mom/sister is prettier than anyone else?	6. I think your mom/sister is very pretty, but I think my mom/sister is very pretty too. (This can always be true because, when you look at someone through the eyes of love, they are always beautiful.) -or- I think God made everyone uniquely

(See questions from adults on the next page.)

© 2003, 2004 Sweet Home Press

Supplemental Materials
S-14

Here are questions that grownups often ask children, along with some tactful answers you might give.

Awkward Questions Grownups Ask	Tactful Answer You Might Give
1. Do you and your sister/brother fight a lot?	1. We don't enjoy fighting -or- We get along well most of the time.
2. Is your brother/sister mean?	2. No. -or- My brother/sister loves me a lot.
3. Is your brother/sister bossy?	3. He/she is very helpful. -or- I appreciate his/her ideas.
4. Is your brother/sister a pain?	4. Occasionally, but I'm sure I'm just as annoying to him/her sometimes. We love each other. -or- He/she is a great brother/sister.
5. Who's best at school? You, or your brother/sister?	5. We both do our best.
6. It's tough living with a teenager isn't it?	6. No -or- My brother/sister and I love each other no matter what age we are.
7. Your mom teaches you at home huh? Is she a mean teacher?	7. My mom loves me and wants me to do my best.
8. Don't you just hate having to take care of your little brother and or sisters?	8. No. -or- Sometimes it's hard, but I know it's worth it.
9. She said no? Aw, mean old mom. Oh well, when you are 18 you don't have to do what they say anymore.	9. I know she wants what's best for me.
10. Do you get spanked a lot? (This isn't exactly a loyalty compromising question, in that it is not necessarily wrong of your parents to spank you often; maybe you needed it. But it probably isn't any of the questioner's business.)	10. Do you think I need more? (with a laugh) (If they persist, say:) My parents do what is best for me, and then go tell your parents about the questioner.

(See questions from children on the previous page.)

© 2003, 2004 Sweet Home Press

Supplemental Materials
S-14

This space is provided so you can write in the left column some of the questions YOU hear from other children. Then write tactful answers in the right column.

Awkward Questions Other Children Ask	Tactful Answers You Might Give

(Write questions from adults on the next page.)

© 2003, 2004 Sweet Home Press

Supplemental Materials

Write in the left column questions that grownups often ask children. Write in the right column some tactful answers you might give.

Awkward Questions Grownups Ask	Tactful Answer You Might Give

(Write questions from children on the previous page.)

© 2003, 2004 Sweet Home Press

Conversation with Character

This material goes with Lesson 15

Please
By Alicia Aspinwall

There was once a little word named "Please, " that lived in a small boy's mouth. Pleases live in everybody's mouth, though people often forget they are there.

Now, all Pleases, to be kept strong and happy, should be taken out of the mouth very often, so they can get air. They are like little fish in a bowl, you know, that come popping up to the top of the water to breathe.

The Please I am going to tell you about lived in the mouth of a boy named Dick; but only once in a long while fif it have a chance to get out. For Dick, I am sorry to say, was a rude little boy; he hardly ever remembered to say "Please."

"Give me some bread! I want some water! Give me that book!"- that is the way he would ask for things.

His father and mother felt very bad about this. And, as for the poor Please itself, it would sit up on the roof of the boy's mouth day after day, hoping for a chance to get out. It was growing weaker and weaker every day.

This boy Dick had a brother, John. Now John was older than Dick-he was almost ten; and he was just as polite as Dick was rude. So his Please had plenty of fresh air, and was strong and happy.

One day at breakfast Dick's Please felt that he *must* have some fresh air, even if he had to run away. So out he ran-out of Dick's mouth- and took a long breath. Then he crept across the table and jumped into John's mouth!

The Please-who-lived-there was very angry.

"Get out!" he cried. "You don't belong here! This is my mouth!"

"I know it." replied Dick's Please. "I live over there in that brother mouth. But alas! I am not happy there. I am never used.

I never get a breath of fresh air! I thought you might be willing to let me stay here for a day or so-until I felt stronger."

"Why, certainly." said the other Please, kindly. " I understand. Stay, of course, and when my master uses me, we will both go out together. He is kind, and I am sure he would not mind saying "Please" twice. Stay, as long as

© 2003, 2004 Sweet Home Press

you like. "

That noon, at dinner, John wanted some butter and this is what he said:

"Father, will you pass me the butter, please-please?"
"Certainly." said the father. "But why be so *very* polite?"

John did not answer. He was turning towards his mother, and said:

"Mother, will you give me a muffin, please-please?"

His mother laughed.

"You shall have the muffin, dear, but why do you say 'please' twice?"

"I don't know." answered John. "The words seem just to jump out, somehow. Katie, please-please, some water!"

This time John was almost frightened.

"Well, well," said his father, "there is no harm done. One can't be too 'pleasing' in this world."

All this time Dick had been calling, "Give me an egg! I want some milk. Give me a spoon!" in the rude way he had. But now he stopped and listened to his brother. He thought it would be fun to try to talk like John, so he began,

"Mother, will you give me a muffin, m-m-m?"

That was all he could say.

So it went on all day, and everyone wondered what was the matter with those two boys. When night came, they were both so tired, and Dick was so cross, that their mother sent them to bed very early.

But the next morning, no sooner had they sat down to breakfast, than Dick's Please ran home again. He had had so much fresh air the day before that now he was feeling quite strong and happy. And the very next moment, he had another airing, for Dick said,

"Father, will you cut my orange, please?" Why the word slipped out as easily as could be! It sounded just as well as when John said it– John was saying only one "please" this morning. And from that time on, Dick was just as polite as his brother.

Supplemental Materials S-21 This material goes with Lesson 21 Conversation with Character

© 2003, 2004 Sweet Home Press

Supplemental Materials
Memorization

This material for use anytime

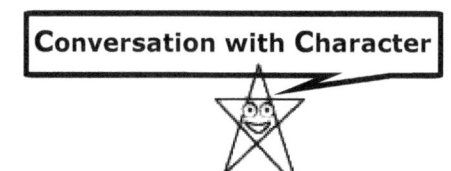

Memorization

Parents: Memorization trains the mind and, if the work memorized is good, trains the heart, as well. Use these supplemental materials to build wisdom, penmanship and good conversation. On the following pages are most of the Bible quotes that appear at the beginning of each chapter.

1. Discuss the meaning of each quote.
2. Cut out all quotes into individual papers, and have your child copy one quote in his or her own handwriting. Hand him or her work on a new quote each day, week, or as you think appropriate.
3. Have the child memorize the quote and recite it at meal time.
4. Encourage your child to use the quote in conversation.

Like this idea? **Quotes with Character** is a book of 201 of quotes from wise people throughout history, just for this purpose. Order this book from Sweet Home Press (sweethomepress.com).

Philippians 2:4	Proverbs 18:2
Do not merely look out for your own personal interests, but also for the interests of others.	A fool does not delight in understanding, But only in revealing his own mind.
Luke 6:31	**Proverbs 1:8-9**
Treat others the same way you want them to treat you.	Hear, my son, your father's instruction And do not forsake your mother's teaching; Indeed, they are a graceful wreath to your head And ornaments about your neck.

© 2003, 2004, 2006 Sweet Home Press

Supplemental Materials
Memorization   This material for use anytime   Conversation with Character

Proverbs 27:2

Let another praise you, and not your own mouth;
A stranger, and not your own lips.

James 1:19

...But everyone must be quick to hear, slow to speak...

James 1:19

...But everyone must be quick to hear, slow to speak...

Proverbs 10:19

When words are many, sin is not absent, but he who holds his tongue is wise.

Numbers 6:24-26

The LORD bless you, and keep you;
The LORD make His face shine on you,
And be gracious to you;
The LORD lift up His countenance on you,
And give you peace.'

Proverbs 6:12-13

A worthless person, a wicked man,
Is the one who walks with a perverse mouth,
Who winks with his eyes, who signals with his feet,
Who points with his fingers.

© 2003, 2004, 2006 Sweet Home Press

Supplemental Materials
Memorization This material for use anytime Conversation with Character

Proverbs 17:28

Even a fool,
when he keeps silent,
is considered wise...

Ephesians 4:2-3

...showing tolerance for one another in love, being diligent to preserve the unity of the Spirit in the bond of peace.

Ecclesiastes 3:1

There is an appointed time for everything...

Proverbs 17:14

The beginning of strife is like letting out water,
So abandon the quarrel before it breaks out.

Proverbs 16:30

He who winks his eyes does so to devise perverse things;
He who compresses his lips brings evil to pass.

Proverbs 11:29

He who brings trouble on his family will inherit only wind, and the fool will be servant to the wise.

© 2003, 2004, 2006 Sweet Home Press

Supplemental Materials
Memorization   This material for use anytime   Conversation with Character

Genesis 50:17

...And now, please forgive the transgression of the servants of the God of your father."
And Joseph wept when they spoke to him.

Deuteronomy 32:1

Give ear, O heavens, and let me speak;
And let the earth hear the words of my mouth.

2 Timothy 4:2

...be ready in season and out of season...

Colossians 4:5

Conduct yourselves with wisdom toward outsiders, making the most of the opportunity.

Proverbs 11:13

He who goes about as a talebearer reveals secrets,
But he who is trustworthy conceals a matter.

Ephesians 6:2-3

Honor your father and mother (which is the first commandment with a promise), so that it may be well with you, and that you may live long on the earth.

© 2003, 2004, 2006 Sweet Home Press

www.ingramcontent.com/pod-product-compliance
Lightning Source LLC
Chambersburg PA
CBHW080438230426
43662CB00015B/2309